P9-DDE-918

TWENTY-SEVEN

ANCIENT CIVILIZATIONS

Ancient Greeks

by Anita Ganeri

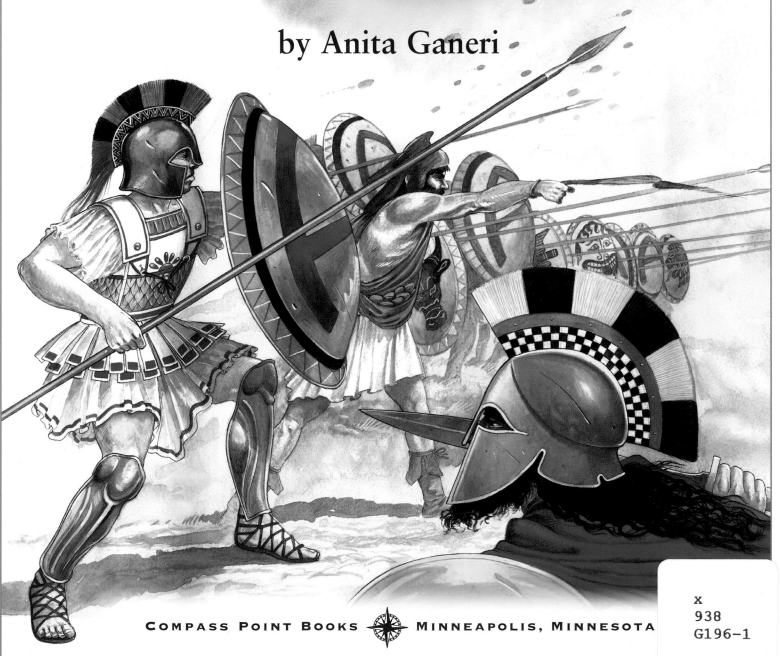

COMPASS POINT BOOKS ✦ MINNEAPOLIS, MINNESOTA

First American edition published in 2006 by
Compass Point Books
3109 West 50th St., #115
Minneapolis, MN 55410

ANCIENT GREEKS
was produced by
David West Children's Books
7 Princeton Court
55 Felsham Road
London SW15 1AZ

Illustrator: Terry Riley
Designer: Gary Jeffrey
Editors: Kate Newport, Nick Healy
Page Production: Bobbie Nuytten
Content Adviser: Sophie J. V. Mills,
  Chair and Associate Professor, Classics Department,
  University of North Carolina Asheville

Visit Compass Point Books on the Internet at
www.compasspointbooks.com
or e-mail your request to
custserv@compasspointbooks.com

Library of Congress Cataloging-in-Publication Data
Ganeri, Anita, 1961-
    Ancient Greeks / by Anita Ganeri.
       p. cm.—(Ancient civilizations)
    Includes bibliographical references and index.
    ISBN 0-7565-1646-3 (hard cover)
    [1. Greece—Civilization—To 146 B.C.—Juvenile literature.] I. Title.
  II. Series: Ancient civilizations (Minneapolis, Minn.)
  DF77.G219 2005
  938—dc22   2005025057

  ISBN 0-7565-1757-5 (paperback)

Contents

The Greeks

Over a period of 2,000 years, the ancient Greeks built one of the greatest civilizations the world has ever seen. At one point in 300 B.C., about 2,300 years ago, the Greek Empire covered an area that stretched far across the Middle East to India.

The Greeks built great cities, produced great thinkers and scientists, and invented democracy. Although the Greeks lived many years ago, we know a lot about their lives.

Look for this man digging up interesting items from the past, like these boards Greek pupils used to practice writing.

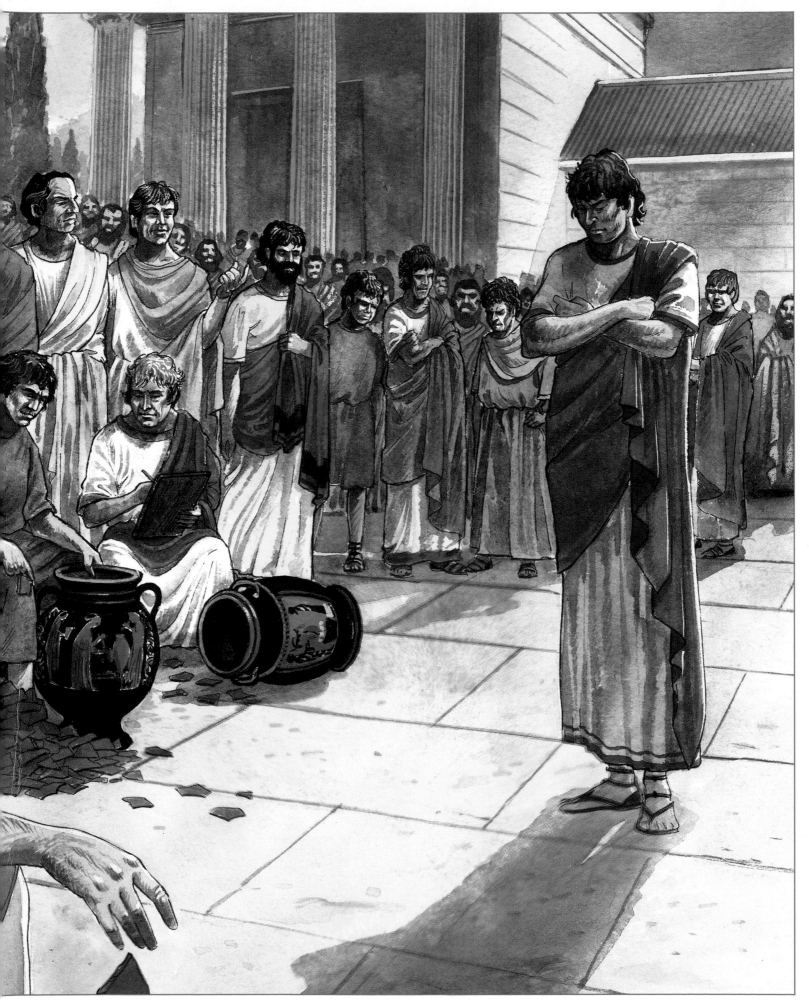

Who Were the First Greeks?

Ancient Greeks were the people who lived in Greece thousands of years ago.

The first great Greek civilization grew on the island of Crete about 4,000 years ago. It was named the Minoan civilization after its famous king, Minos. The Minoans were very good at arts and crafts. They were also great traders, which made them wealthy.

Minoan towns were built around palaces, such as the one at a place called Knossos. About 30,000 people are thought to have lived in and around the palace.

Wall paintings from Knossos show the sport of bull-leaping. Teams of young men grabbed a bull's horns and leaped onto its back.

Many things have been found on the sites of Minoan towns. These items have helped to build a picture of what Minoan life was like. The design on a golden cup tells us about Minoan bull-leaping.

Greek myth tells of a terrible monster—half-man, half-bull—that lived in a labyrinth, or maze, on Crete. He was called the Minotaur. Each year, young girls and boys were sent into the labyrinth, where the Minotaur might eat them or they might get lost and die.

The Greek World

Greece is made up of hundreds of islands in the Mediterranean Sea and a mainland that has lots of mountains.

In ancient times, parts of present-day Italy and Turkey were inhabited by Greeks. Many Greeks went there to get away from crowding and to find better land to farm.

About 3,000 years ago, the Mycenaean people ruled mainland Greece. They built huge hilltop cities, with thick stone walls around them.

The golden age for Greece was the Classical Period, about 2,500 years ago. The Greeks defeated their arch enemy, the mighty Persians, and at home they made strides in art and academics.

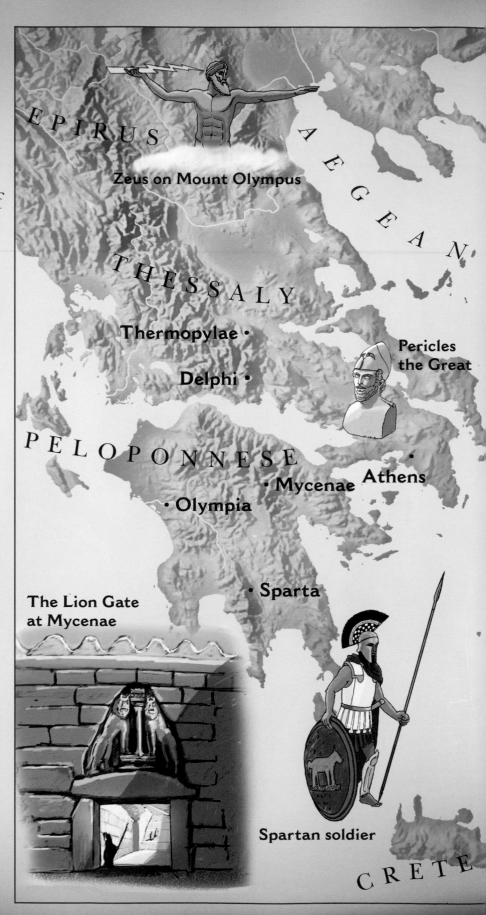

EPIRUS

Zeus on Mount Olympus

AEGEAN

THESSALY

Thermopylae •

Delphi •

Pericles the Great

PELOPONNESE

• Olympia

• Mycenae

Athens

• Sparta

The Lion Gate at Mycenae

Spartan soldier

CRETE

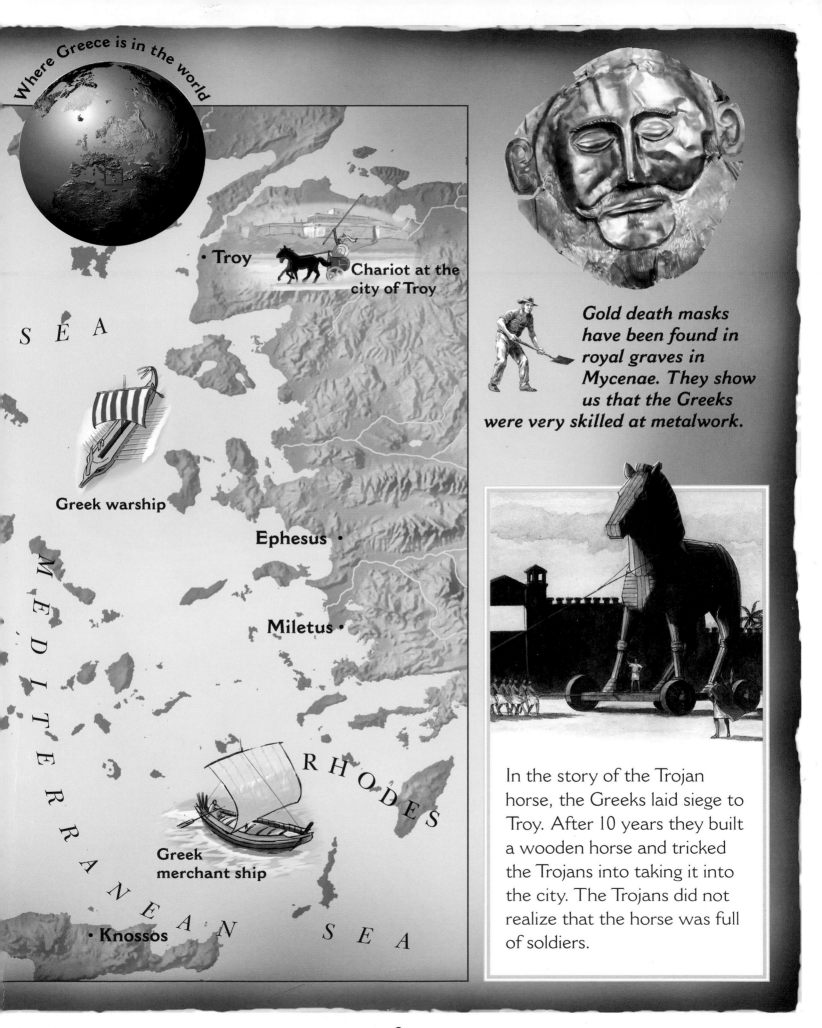

• Troy

Chariot at the city of Troy

S E A

Greek warship

M E D I T E R R A N E A N   S E A

Ephesus •

Miletus •

R H O D E S

Greek merchant ship

• Knossos

Gold death masks have been found in royal graves in Mycenae. They show us that the Greeks were very skilled at metalwork.

In the story of the Trojan horse, the Greeks laid siege to Troy. After 10 years they built a wooden horse and tricked the Trojans into taking it into the city. The Trojans did not realize that the horse was full of soldiers.

Athens and Sparta

In ancient times, Greece was not one big country like it is today. It was divided into many small city-states. Each was made up of a city and the country around it, and had its own rulers, armies, and coins.

The two leading city-states were Athens and Sparta. They were bitter enemies. This rivalry stopped briefly when their armies joined to defeat the Persians about 2,500 years ago. But the peace did not last. About 50 years later, the Peloponnesian Wars broke out between the two and lasted for 27 years.

Greek foot soldiers were called hoplites.
They wore bronze helmets and
armor, and carried a short sword,
a long spear, and a shield.

In Sparta, anybody who was thought to be a coward was punished. Boys were even taught to steal because it made them brave and clever.

The Spartans were famous as the toughest warriors in Greece. At 7, boys were sent off to army camp, where demanding training made their lives difficult.

Family Life

In Ancient Greece, the father was the head of the family. He was in charge of his wife, his children, and any slaves.

Women had little freedom. Girls would get married when they were about 15 years old. Then they would spend their lives running the home and looking after their children.

Greek children from rich families had many toys to play with. They had clay dolls with jointed arms and legs, spinning tops, and clay rattles in the shape of owls and pigs.

Slaves were often prisoners of war. They were then sold at market by slavetraders. Wealthy families had many slaves to look after them and do their work.

At about the age of 12 or 13, Greek children became adults. To show that they were leaving childhood behind, they had to stop playing with their toys and give them to the god Apollo. This was done at a special ceremony in the temple.

A pot shows the importance of parenting and childhood in Greek times. Greeks cherished children because they would carry on the family. Sons were valued more because they would inherit money and property.

Country and City

Most ancient Greeks were farmers. The mountains and the dry weather made growing food hard work. Only strong plants, such as some grains, grapes, and olives, could be grown. Many farmers also kept sheep and goats for their meat and milk.

Most Greeks grew all the food they needed on their farms. They ate a simple diet of bread, porridge, olives, vegetables, figs, and cheese. Rich people ate more meat and fish.

Most of the olives grown were crushed in an olive press to make oil. Olive oil was very important. It was used for cooking, lighting, and for makeup.

Wine made from grapes was the most popular drink in Ancient Greece. It was stored in pots called amphorae (above).

Greek houses, both in the city and countryside, were simple buildings, made from mud bricks dried in the sunshine. They were built around a courtyard with rooms leading off it. Rich families had more rooms than poor families did.

Bedroom

Central courtyard

Main doorway

Going to School

Greek boys went to school from the age of 7. If their parents were rich, they might stay at school until they were 18, when they started their army training. To the ancient Greeks, keeping fit was just as important as doing lessons.

Pupils practiced writing the Greek alphabet on wooden boards covered with wax. They wrote with a pointed metal pen called a stylus.

A rich family often used a slave to take their son to school. The slave stayed with the boy during all of his classes to watch him and make sure that he behaved himself properly.

At school, boys studied subjects such as reading, writing, mathematics, music, poetry, and athletics.

Later, they were taught how to speak in public, and studied politics, science, and philosophy.

Girls and children from poor families did not go to school. Girls stayed at home with their mothers and learned how to spin, weave, and run the household.

Great Greek Thinkers

The Greeks were great thinkers. Many of their ideas still help us today.

Greek philosophers, or "lovers of knowledge," such as Aristotle, Plato, and Socrates, were some of the first to ask questions about the world around them and try to make sense of it. Ancient Greeks were also very good scientists, inventors, and mathematicians. Many of their discoveries provide the basis for scientific work today.

For example, Pythagoras and Archimedes were the first people to figure out many basic rules of mathematics.

Greek philosophers and their students met in gymnasia. They were not only centers for sports, but also for learning. They had libraries and classrooms as well as training grounds.

A story says that the scientist Archimedes had his greatest idea in the bathtub. He was able to figure out how much space an object takes up by placing it in water.

Pythagoras was born on the island of Samos and is famous for figuring out rules about shapes.

Having Fun

Going to the theater and playing sports were very important in ancient Greece. Theater started when songs were performed as part of holy festivals. These grew into plays. Open-air theaters were built all over Greece. Crowds of 18,000 people could fit into many of the theaters.

Men played all the parts in a Greek play. Women were not allowed to be actors. Some actors played the main roles. Others sang and danced in a group called the chorus.

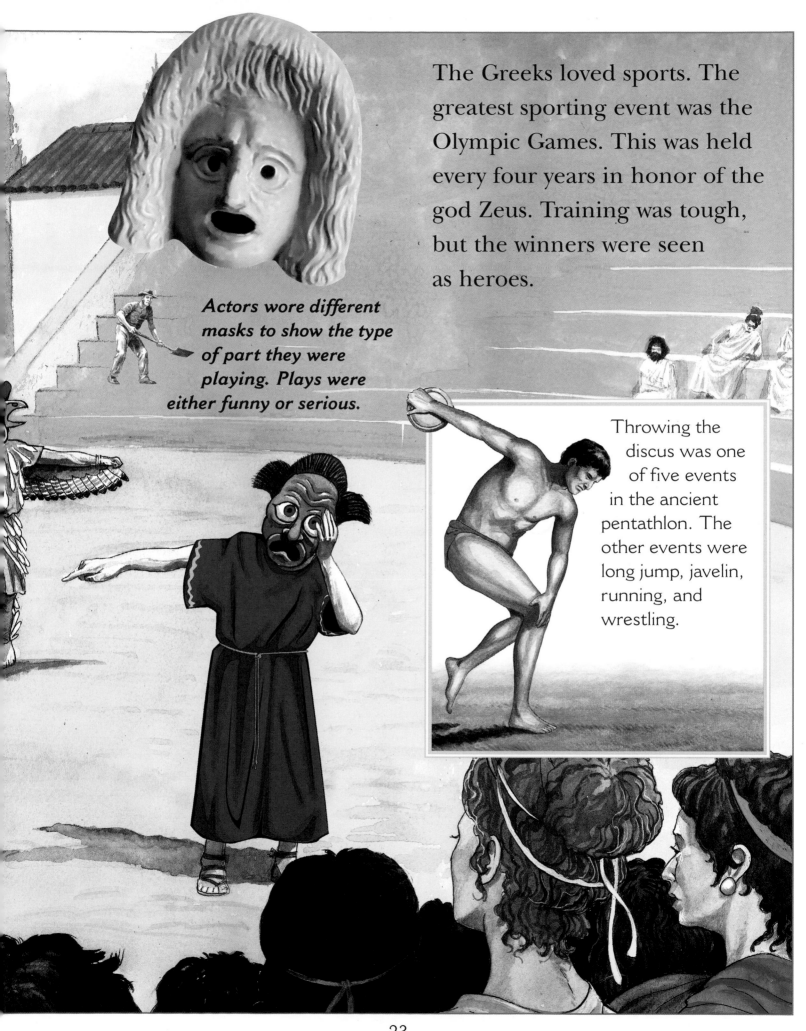

The Greeks loved sports. The greatest sporting event was the Olympic Games. This was held every four years in honor of the god Zeus. Training was tough, but the winners were seen as heroes.

Actors wore different masks to show the type of part they were playing. Plays were either funny or serious.

Throwing the discus was one of five events in the ancient pentathlon. The other events were long jump, javelin, running, and wrestling.

Gods and Goddesses

Ancient Greeks worshipped many gods and goddesses. They believed that the gods watched over them and looked after every part of the world, life, and death. The gods could not die and were very powerful. The Greeks showed them great respect.

The most important gods were the Olympians, who were believed to live on Mount Olympus in Greece. Zeus was king of the gods and god of the sky. His wife, Hera, was goddess of women.

1. **Zeus**—*king of the gods*
2. **Hera**—*queen of the gods*
3. **Apollo**—*god of the sun and healing*
4. **Artemis**—*goddess of the moon and hunting*
5. **Poseidon**—*god of the sea*
6. **Ares**—*god of war*
7. **Athena**—*goddess of wisdom and war*

The Greeks built many great temples. These were the gods' homes on Earth. Inside a temple stood a statue of the god for whom the temple was built. Sacrifices and offerings were made there in honor of the gods.

The Parthenon in Athens was a temple built to honor Athena, goddess of wisdom and war. She was also goddess of the city.

8. **Pluto and Persephone**—*king and queen of the underworld*
9. **Hermes**—*messenger of the gods*
10. **Hephaestos**—*god of fire and metalwork*
11. **Hestia**—*goddess of the hearth and home*
12. **Dionysus**—*god of wine*
13. **Demeter**—*goddess of plants and farming*
14. **Aphrodite**—*goddess of love*

The Greeks went to holy places, called oracles, to ask the gods about the future. The most famous oracle was the one at Delphi.

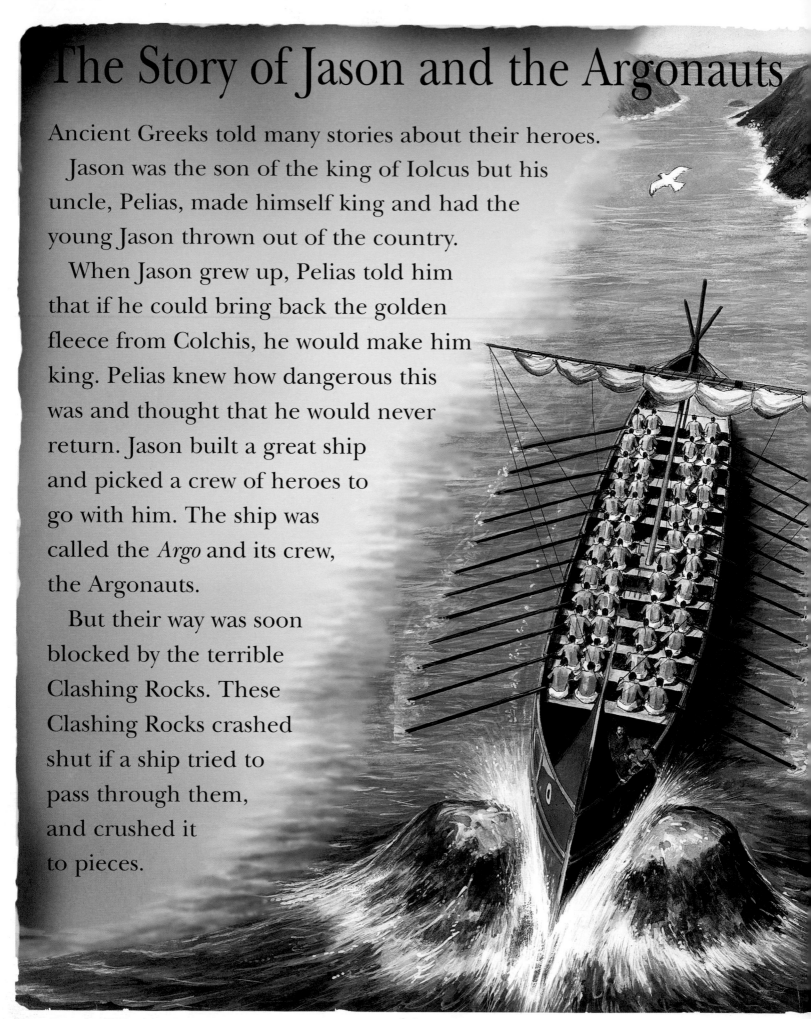

The Story of Jason and the Argonauts

Ancient Greeks told many stories about their heroes.

Jason was the son of the king of Iolcus but his uncle, Pelias, made himself king and had the young Jason thrown out of the country.

When Jason grew up, Pelias told him that if he could bring back the golden fleece from Colchis, he would make him king. Pelias knew how dangerous this was and thought that he would never return. Jason built a great ship and picked a crew of heroes to go with him. The ship was called the *Argo* and its crew, the Argonauts.

But their way was soon blocked by the terrible Clashing Rocks. These Clashing Rocks crashed shut if a ship tried to pass through them, and crushed it to pieces.

The local king told Jason to send a bird through first to make the rocks crash shut. Then, when they opened again, the Argonauts quickly rowed through.

When they reached Colchis, the king gave Jason a test. Jason had to plow a field with two fire-breathing bulls and plant some dragon's teeth. When Jason did this, soldiers grew from the teeth and attacked him. The king's daughter, Medea, helped him to protect himself and to deal with the fierce dragon that guarded the golden fleece. She had Orpheus play a lullaby to put the dragon to sleep. While the dragon slept, Jason took the golden fleece, hurried back to the *Argo*, and sailed back to Iolcus.

What Happened to the Greeks?

About 2,300 years ago the Macedonians, who lived north of Greece, became very rich and powerful. The most famous Macedonian king was Alexander the Great. When he died at age 32, he ruled the largest empire that the ancient world had ever known.

When Alexander became king he was only 20 years old. He was a great soldier, and quickly took over Persia, Egypt, Babylon, and parts of India.

When Alexander died, his empire was split between his generals. Only 200 years later, Greece was taken over by the Romans. The Greeks continued to rule in Egypt, but after a while Egypt too became part of the Roman empire.

The Romans looked up to the Greeks and borrowed many Greek ideas. They even made copies of Greek poems and statues.

Throughout his empire, Alexander built many new cities which he named Alexandria. The most famous was in Egypt. That city's huge lighthouse was one of the seven wonders of the ancient world.

29

Glossary

amphorae—large two-handled pots used to store oil and wine

citizens—men born in a city-state who were not slaves

city-state—a Greek city and the surrounding countryside

democracy—a form of government in which the people elect their leaders

empire—a large state made up of many countries, all ruled by a leader called an emperor

gymnasia—sports centers that also became centers of learning

hoplites—Greek foot soldiers

labyrinth—a maze of winding passages that is difficult to find the way out of

metics—men born outside a city-state who were not slaves

oracles—holy places where people went to consult a god, through a priest or priestess

ostraka—(singular: ostrakon) pieces of pottery on which the names of unpopular politicians were written

philosophy—a love of knowledge

politician—a person who is part of, or seeks to be part of, government

trade—buying and selling of goods such as jewelry and food

tyrant—a ruler who had absolute power and control

Further Resources

AT THE LIBRARY

Covert, Kim. *Ancient Greece*. Mankato, Minn.: Capstone Press, 2004.

Hovey, Kate. *Voices of the Trojan War*. New York: Margaret K. McElderry, 2004.

Lassieur, Allison. *The Ancient Greeks*. New York: Franklin Watts, 2004.

ON THE WEB

For more information on *Ancient Greeks,* use FactHound
to track down Web sites related to this book.

1. Go to *www.facthound.com*
2. Type in a search word related to this book
    or this book ID: 0756516463
3. Click on the *Fetch It* button.

FactHound will find the best Web sites for you.

LOOK FOR MORE BOOKS IN THIS SERIES

ANCIENT MAYA
ISBN 0-7565-1677-3

ANCIENT ROMANS
ISBN 0-7565-1644-7

THE VIKINGS
ISBN 0-7565-1678-1

Index